LONDON BUSES
around Kent

Roy Hobbs

Ian Allan PUBLISHING

Front cover: RT2675 on route 146 from Bromley heads for Keston (Fox) along Baston Road during June 1969, this being a short working of the normal run to the picturesque village of Downe. *Michael Allen*

Back cover: As a London Country AF waits in Westerham's Market Square on route 410 from Bromley to Reigate, RF663 on a connecting 483 service is about to depart for Tonbridge station on 30 June 1975. This latter route was a part replacement for the 403 (Wallington–Tonbridge) service, shortened in July 1971 to terminate at Chelsham. *Michael Furnell*

Title page: Standing at the Farnborough (George) terminus of route 229 on a summer evening in August 1978, RM255 awaits its return to Bexleyheath garage on a Sidcup (SP) duty. Now registered HVS 935, this bus was last recorded as being in the care of a Hertford company, following initial disposal in January 1988. *Roy Hobbs*

Left: Against a misty North Downs background, RT4747 makes its turn at the quaintly named Noah's Ark terminus of route 421 near Kemsing on 18 December 1971. This unusual name is believed to stem from a time when the still-existing 17th-century Noah's Ark Cottage and its adjacent land, due to an elevated position, provided a haven for livestock when the nearby fields were regularly flooded by a natural spring. *Michael Allen*

First published 2006

ISBN (10) 0 7110 3112 6
ISBN (13) 978 0 7110 3112 8

Published by Ian Allan Publishing

an imprint of Ian Allan Publishing Ltd, Hersham, Surrey KT12 4RG.
Printed in England by Ian Allan Printing Ltd, Hersham, Surrey KT12 4RG.

Code: 0607/B2

Visit the Ian Allan Publishing website at www.ianallanpublishing.com

Introduction

As with the previous Surrey album, details of the first public transport services in that part of Kent later to be served by London Transport (LT) are difficult to find, but a record exists of an early horse-bus service; this was the Tunbridge Wells, Southborough & District Omnibus Co (incorporated April 1896), taken over from an earlier operator, which effectively ran between these points until September 1911 when it was forced into liquidation through financial difficulties.

The East Surrey Traction Co, formed in Reigate in March 1911, entered the scene in April 1914, when route expansion saw its route 24 (Reigate–Godstone Green) extended to Sevenoaks (Tubs Hill) via Westerham and Chipstead, becoming its first entry into the county. Prior to this Autocar Services Ltd of Tunbridge Wells, formed in 1909, had started a motor-bus service between that town and Southborough. In August 1919 a new route was introduced direct to Sevenoaks, this being extended the following November to Farnborough, where it connected with the London General Omnibus Co (LGOC) route 47 to Shoreditch; a precursor to the July 1921 agreement between the LGOC and East Surrey resulted in the latter's takeover in May from Autocar of the Sevenoaks–Farnborough section, this being extended to Bromley North station in August 1921, adopting route number S2 (later 402).

Co-operation concerning various aspects had existed between the LGOC and East Surrey since 1914, and it was also agreed in July 1921 that the latter would have responsibility for services in the Cray Valley and into Dartford; this was followed in April 1928 by both concerns' taking a controlling interest in Autocar, by then operating close on 100 vehicles in West Kent and East Sussex. At this point it should be

recorded that there were also a number of small independent companies operating in the area, especially around Sevenoaks and Dartford, to which reference is made in the appropriate captions.

A number of services in the counties north of London were transferred to East Surrey control in December 1931, resulting in the original title becoming unsuitable, and the name was consequently changed to London General Country Services Ltd. However, this organisation was destined to have a rather short life, as it was compulsorily acquired by the London Passenger Transport Board (LPTB) on 1 July 1933 under the Act of that year, the original East Surrey territory becoming the Southern Area of the Country Bus & Coach Department.

With the new arrangement further territorial adjustments took effect, and Autocar routes outside the LPTB boundary were hived off, Maidstone & District Motor Services then becoming responsible for management of the company; this was counterbalanced to some extent by M&D's loss to the Board of routes, 55 vehicles and two garages in the Dartford and Gravesend areas. Other than the acquisition of further independents, including six in the Gravesend area in 1934, there were

Merlin MB315 on route 126 picks up a further batch of passengers in a bustling Bromley High Street during June 1974. Operating at this time between Beckenham Junction and Eltham (Well Hall station), these OMO single-deckers had replaced the RT type here in October 1968. 'Merlin' was the name adopted by LT for this type, which in reality was an AEC Swift. *John Bishop*

few immediate route changes, although the area scheme was introduced in the Dartford, Swanley and Gravesend districts in May 1934.

Attention was now to be concentrated on investment to build up a more standardised fleet, in view of the wide diversity of vehicle types inherited at the amalgamation. There had been a close association between the LGOC and the Associated Equipment Co Ltd (AEC) since 1912, when the latter was formed to take over the LGOC's vehicle-building works at Walthamstow, although production was later transferred to Southall. An extremely significant development was the appearance in July 1929 of the AEC Regent chassis, which represented a quantum leap in bus design. One of the first pre-production examples, fitted with a 51-seat double-deck body by Short Bros, entered service with Autocar in August 1929 and was accepted into LGOC stock the following December. After its return to Chiswick Works in March 1930 it was transferred to East Surrey and remained in the Country Area fleet until withdrawal in 1948.

The AEC Regent, along with its single-deck counterpart, the Regal, became the standard for the LPTB for several years up to World War 2. Known respectively as the ST and T classes, these were progressively improved over succeeding years as the later STL and 10T10 types, culminating in the introduction in 1939 of the RT-type double-decker. Over this period, Chiswick Works, under its LGOC and LPTB owners, had been responsible for body design, which had resulted in vehicles of particularly handsome proportions.

Following World War 2 progressive development of the RT design, with further body improvements, resulted in a vehicle which, with Leyland variants, was to serve both Central and Country areas for in excess of 30 years. Single-deck development proceeded in a somewhat different direction, with a front-entrance type, featuring an underfloor engine, which would be employed in both bus and coach use. Known as the RF, this first appeared in 1952 and similarly became a fleet standard, the final withdrawals occurring only in 1979 — the same year as those of the RT.

In the 1950s, continuing a policy of progressive improvement, engineers at both LT and AEC embarked upon designing a successor to the RT which could also be used for trolleybus replacement. The result was the Routemaster, or RM, which employed a form of chassisless construction, incorporating subframes. The first production examples entered service in the Central Area in 1959, to be followed by a coach version, the RMC, for Green Line use and the longer RML for both Central and Country areas, together with its coach equivalent, the RCL. These have more than proved their worth in London service, many having achieved close on 50 years of operation. Although the last examples in normal service have now been retired, a few are retained for two so-called 'heritage' routes in Central London.

Upon transfer to the National Bus Company (NBC) in January 1970 the Country Bus & Coach Department became London Country Bus Services Ltd (LCBS). Deregulation in October 1986 prompted further separation into four independent units, each of which has since been absorbed into other dominant national groups. Privatisation of London Buses (the former Central Area) took

As the driver of RF194 prepares to leave Northfleet (NF) garage to take up a working on Green Line route 701 (Gravesend–Ascot) on 22 June 1975, RMLs 2309 and 2342 and BN30 (Bristol LHS6L/ECW) await their next rostered turns on routes 480, 488 and 490 respectively. These indicate the variety of liveries that could be found across the fleet at this time. *R. C. Riley*

place in 1994/5, and nine of the companies formed in readiness continue to provide the majority of services, overall control being in the hands of Transport for London (TfL).

In compiling this collection I have again taken the pre-1964 GLC boundary as a definition of the county limits, allowing the inclusion of such locations as Bromley, Chislehurst, Welling etc. An attempt has been made to concentrate mainly on the period through the 1960s up to around 1980, to provide a flavour of the period before too many irrevocable changes had taken place, although a few later views have been included for comparison purposes. Where possible I have endeavoured to show the various vehicles in the context of their surroundings, many of which have changed considerably in the 25 or more years that have elapsed since the photographs were taken. As previously, the subject has been dealt with chronologically.

Several photographers have again been kind enough to submit their irreplaceable transparencies for use in this publication, these including Michael Allen, John Bishop, Dave Brown, Michael Furnell, Bruce Jenkins, Gerald Mead, Dick Riley, Geoff Rixon and James Whiting of Capital Transport; my thanks also to D. Trevor Rowe for the use of material by the late Lyndon Rowe. Special mention must also be made of the assistance given by Michael Furnell concerning the detailed information provided for a number of the locations featured, whilst David Ruddom of the London Historical Research Group of the Omnibus Society has once more been extremely helpful in unravelling the intricacies of some of the routes involved.

It would have been impossible to produce this album without assistance from other written sources, and I would particularly single out the following from which much useful and historical information has

been obtained. *The Motorbus in London Country* by Kenneth Warren (published by Ian Allan in 1984) proved a mine of information, as did *East Surrey* by Reg Durrant, John King and George Robbins (HJ Publications, 1974); reference was also made to *Bus Portfolio 3: RFs* by Steve Fennell (World of Transport, 1988), to *London Buses in the 1960s* by Ken Glazier (Capital Transport, 1998) and to *London Country* by Laurie Akehurst and David Stewart (Capital Transport, 2001), as well as to the various publications produced by the London Omnibus Traction Society (LOTS), especially the quarterly *London Bus Magazine* and the *London Bus Review* issued annually since 1973, in various forms.

Finally, my apologies in advance for any errors or discrepancies that may appear in the final text, as these will be mine alone.

Roy Hobbs
Exeter
May 2006

Awaiting its return to Northfleet, RT621 is seen on the King's Farm Estate stand at Gravesend on 4 May 1963 on route 496. The use of upper-case lettering on the intermediate blind will be noted, this style having generally been phased out from 1961 onwards. Originally fitted with a roofbox body, this bus had been amongst the first deliveries of the type to the Country Area, being allocated originally to Hemel Hempstead (HH) garage for routes 302, 314 and 316 in August 1948. Following conversion of route 496 to RML operation in May 1966, the next change occurred in October 1972, when these were replaced by MBS one-man-operated (OMO) single-deckers, employing the farebox system with flat fares of 5p (adults) and 4p (children). This was abandoned in December 1981 and replaced with conventional fare-collection methods. *Gerald Mead*

Above: During 1964 LT provided two services from Essex into Kent via the Dartford Tunnel: bus route 300 (Stifford Clays–Dartford) and Green Line 722, which had been extended from Upminster (Corbets Tey) to Dartford in 1963. The latter extension was withdrawn in November 1964, whilst the 300 was cut back to Grays in June 1965. Both had been double-deck services. Replacement came in the form of route 399, using a GS (Guy Special) 26-seat OMO single-decker running from Grays (GY) garage and more appropriate to the available traffic. However, due mainly to the operating losses incurred through Tunnel tolls, it would itself be withdrawn in May 1967. Awaiting its return journey, GS28 stands outside Dartford Public Library during June 1965. This bus was last recorded as being privately preserved with an owner in Chirbury, Shropshire. *John Bishop*

Right: Another example of this 84-strong class, GS56, departs the Orpington Station terminus of route 471 in March 1966. This was a circular service linking various village communities to the south of Orpington with the town. Based on a modified Guy Vixen chassis, the 26-seat GS was the smallest type then operating in London Transport's Country Area, having been introduced in 1953 mainly to replace the C type (Leyland Cub), dating from the 1930s, on restricted and lightly trafficked routes in rural districts. Now with private owners, GS56 was last reported as being located in Southborough. *James Whiting*

During 1965, with the upgrading of various bus and coach routes in the Country Area to Routemaster operation, the opportunity was taken to paint displaced RTs in red livery for transfer to the Central Area; this was in order to hasten the withdrawal from the fleet of the Leyland RTL and RTW variants. However, this produced its own shortage in the Country Area, with the result that a number had to remain in service, although repainted, until the next delivery of RMLs; this took place in May 1966, when Northfleet (NF) routes 488, 495 and 496 were converted. RT3048 waits at the King's Farm Estate stand on a 488 duty on 30 April 1966, shortly before transfer. Use of red buses on route 480 was prohibited, due to its entering the Central Area. *Gerald Mead*

In January 1972, London Country introduced a number of service changes, especially in the Gravesend area, where uneconomic parts of the network were reduced or withdrawn due to a lack of financial support from local authorities. This resulted in the withdrawal of route 451 to Hartley Court via Betsham, as compared with the more direct route 490. GS36 is seen in Peacock Street, Gravesend, on a working to Hartley Court in May 1967. Following conversion of the 451 and 490 to RF operation in October 1969, the only GS-operated route was to be found north of the Thames, the 336A (Rickmansworth–Loudwater Village) continuing thus until March 1972. The stand in Peacock Street is no longer used by local services. *John Bishop*

Also seen waiting on the Peacock Street, Gravesend, stand used by workings to Gravesend (Clock Tower) is RF673, on route 489 to Ash (White Swan) during June 1967. In January 1972 this route was renumbered 490A, presumably to facilitate interworking with the 490, but in July 1973 it reverted to its original number — without, one hopes, causing too much confusion amongst the local populace! In September 1974 the 450/489/490 group of routes received new BN (Bristol LHS6L) single-deckers, replacing the RFs used up to that time. Delivered in September 1953, RF673 was amongst the final members of this 700-strong class, remaining in service until February 1976. It was last recorded as being in a private collection with five others of the type, based in Hertfordshire. *John Bishop*

In August 1968, probably on a Sunday, two schoolboy cyclists eagerly check their route map outside Swanley Junction (SJ) garage whilst a collection of buses await their next turn of duty. These include red RT1117 on route 21A, together with green RTs 2817 and 3442. The garage has an interesting if somewhat chequered history. The last remaining of five garages constructed by the LGOC on behalf of East Surrey in the 1920s, it was opened in October 1925 to house 16 vehicles. Closed by London Country in January 1986, it was reopened that August to service the vehicles required to operate route 51 (Orpington–Woolwich), gained on tender from London Regional Transport (LRT). Closed again in August 1989 upon the transfer of operations to Dartford (DT), it reopened temporarily from December 1995 to March 1996 for Orpington Buses. Final occupation was by Southlands Travel, between August 1998 and December 2004. At the time of writing the now rather dilapidated premises were being offered for rental, specifically for use by a transport company. *Michael Allen*

Above: On the same date as the previous illustration, RT3886 heads north along the wide expanse of London Road, Swanley, on a short working of route 423 via Dartford to Watchgate (Ladywood Road), in the latter town's Darenth area. Nowadays this service originates in Dartford and is extended to New Ash Green, rather than terminating in Longfield, and serves the Bluewater shopping complex and the Darent Valley Hospital. RT3886 would be sold in September 1972 to a dealer in Ewell, Surrey, and exported to British Columbia, Canada, the following January, last being reported with a charitable organisation in December 1994. *Michael Allen*

Right: In the immediate postwar era route 21 operated between Farningham and Moorgate, whilst the 21A variation diverted at Eltham for Woolwich.

From October 1956 the 21 ended at Sidcup on weekdays, Farningham journeys being reduced to Sundays only; journeys on the 21A, which outside peak hours had been cut back as a Sidcup–Eltham (Well Hall station) service, were now extended back to Farningham. In June 1968 the remaining weekend journeys on the 21 were withdrawn, the 21A now being shortened to end at Swanley (SJ) garage, apart from odd peak-hour workings. However, a weekend 21A service from Sidcup was introduced in replacement, RT1117 being seen in Sidcup High Street in August 1968. The RTs would be superseded by MB-type OMO single-deckers that October. The 21A would finally be withdrawn altogether in October 1984, replaced by route 233; currently this is operated by Metrobus, with Dennis Dart SLF single-deckers. *Michael Allen*

A trio of RFs line up at the well-known location of Station Approach, Orpington, on a variety of services on 25 January 1969; RFs 222 and 634 are shown respectively on routes 471 and 431, whilst RF187 awaits its next journey on route 493. The varying types of blind display will be noted. Former Green Line coaches RFs 187 and 222 were to remain in service until January 1976 and May 1975 respectively, but RF634 would be withdrawn in October 1974. Renumbered R5 and R6 respectively, routes 471 (illustrated on page 7) and 431 would become part of Orpington's original Roundabout scheme in August 1986, the 493 losing its Chelsfield section to new local service R3 and in 1996 becoming new R9; subsequent re-tendering has seen operator changes and, in March 1988, the loss of the original R6, but the R3 and R5 remain, with some variations. *Michael Allen*

Orpington station terminus is again featured on the same date as previously with RT2757 on route 229 to Woolwich (Parsons Hill); in the background RF187 waits to return to Green Street Green on the 493. This location still serves as a terminus, for route 51 to Woolwich, the 477 to Dartford and the R5 Orpington circular. Upon the withdrawal of the Woolwich–Bexleyheath section in May 1977 the 229 was re-routed from Orpington to terminate at Farnborough (George), utilising the RM type operating from Sidcup (SP) garage. Go-Ahead subsidiary London Central, using Volvo B7TL/Plaxton low-floor double-deckers working from Bexleyheath (BX) garage, is currently responsible for this service. RT2757 met its fate in February 1974, when it was sold to a breaker in the Barnsley area. *Michael Allen*

Above: The small town of Westerham was originally well-known as an interchange point for various Country Area routes, all scheduled to arrive within minutes of each other, allowing convenient connections for those heading in the Bromley, Croydon and Sevenoaks directions. RT983, on route 403 to Tonbridge station, passes through a snowy town centre on 8 February 1969, alongside the green (with the statue of famous former resident General Wolfe just out of sight to the right). Route 403 would later be curtailed to terminate at Chelsham, being replaced in July 1971 by the 403A, later the 483, which ran until May 1987; currently there is no direct link between Chelsham and Westerham, although Metrobus route 401 provides the service eastwards from the town and now completes its journey at Tunbridge Wells. *Michael Allen*

Right: Seen picking up its (predominantly) shopper passengers outside the parade opposite Longfield station, a well-patronised GS36 is pictured on a 490 journey to Hartley Court on 13 March 1969. The GS (Guy Special) type, as mentioned previously, utilised a basic Guy Vixen chassis, with some Otter parts, and featured a distinctive bonnet assembly based on that designed for the Ford Thames lorry. The bodywork was by Eastern Coach Works and followed broadly LT practice, other than using the Lowestoft builder's internal fittings and, notably, incorporating sliding window vents rather than those of the wind-down variety. The 490 would be withdrawn from Hartley Court and diverted to New Ash Green in July 1973, by which time the route had been converted to RF operation. GS36 was last recorded as being with a private owner in Bournemouth. *Michael Allen*

Left: As its crew take a rest break between duties on route 138, RT3744 stands amidst the silver birches in the residential suburb of Coney Hall, near Hayes, on 3 May 1969 before returning to the less tranquil streets of Bromley and its North Station terminus. Route 138, in this form, was introduced in November 1940, when service 232 was double-decked and renumbered accordingly. Operation around this period was with STLs from Bromley (TB) garage, which were temporarily reinforced early in 1950 by hired Leeds Corporation AEC Regents, these being mechanically similar. Both types were replaced in June 1950 by 8ft-wide Leyland RTWs, which remained only until February 1951 when RTs took over; these operated the service until 10 May 1969, when OMO operation was introduced using MB single-deckers. After a period with Kentish Bus in the early 1990s the route was taken over by Metrobus, which currently employs short Dennis Darts based at its Orpington depot. *Michael Allen*

Above: The village of Wrotham is the location for this June 1969 photograph featuring the daily conjunction of Green Line route 719 and service 423, both of which terminated here. RF123, one of the type modernised in March 1967, awaits its return working to Hemel Hempstead, whilst RT599 is due to depart for Longfield station, south of Dartford. The RT originally had a body with a roof-mounted route-number box, being one of the first four of its type to be painted green for Country Area service — from Tring (TG) garage on route 301 — in July 1948. In April 1978 route 719 was diverted away from Wrotham to terminate at East Grinstead, replacing the southern leg of route 708 from Victoria; substitution, albeit only until July 1980, was provided by route 729, running single peak-hour journeys in each direction to/from the Maidstone & District depot at Borough Green. Wrotham is no longer a terminus, the 423 having also been cut back, to West Kingsdown, in April 1978. *Dave Brown*

Above: Photographed a short distance over the original London/Kent boundary, RT793 waits at the now-demolished Eltham Well Hall station before commencing the return working of predominantly Kent route 228 to Chislehurst via Sidcup on 14 June 1969. The RT type was replaced on the 228 by MB-type single-deckers on Sundays from October 1969, weekday conversion to RMs being effected in May 1977. Latterly operated by Kentish Bus, the route was withdrawn in September 1996 and is now partly covered by routes 160 (Catford–Sidcup) and 162 (Eltham–Beckenham Junction), the former operated by Stagecoach Selkent and the latter by Arriva Kent Thameside, employing short versions of the Dennis Trident double-decker and Dennis Dart single-decker respectively. *Lyndon Rowe*

Right: Judging by the absence of people in one of Bromley's usually crowded thoroughfares, this view would appear to have been recorded some time after shop closing. RT3844 waits in the High Street on 21 June 1969 while on route 61 to Eltham (Well Hall station). This illustration is of particular interest in that RT3844 is fitted with one of the 300 early 'roofbox' bodies, produced as a stopgap in 1949 by Saunders Engineering Co of Anglesey, due to delivery delays by regular suppliers Park Royal and Weymann. Being of non-standard design, these became early candidates for disposal, all buses so fitted, including isolated non-revenue-earning examples, being withdrawn by January 1971; the final example, RT3062, which had been converted as a mobile instruction unit, was subsequently purchased by Ensignbus for its 'working museum' fleet. Shortened to terminate at Chislehurst (Gordon Arms), route 61 is now operated by First London with VN (Volvo B7TL) low-floor double-deckers. *Michael Allen*

Left: RML2349 waits on its stand at Bromley North station during July 1969 on a short working on route 410, returning to Godstone garage rather than travelling the full length of the route to Reigate. The Godstone-based RMLs were the first of their type allocated to Country Area services, in October 1965. However, because insufficient green vehicles were available by the time of the related timetable change, a number of red examples were provided for short periods to cover the 409/410/411 group of routes, replacing the RTs that had been operating on the 410 since the previous November. The RTs had themselves displaced the RLH-class lowbridge buses employed on the service from July 1950, this being achieved by dint of diverting the route to by-pass Oxted town centre, until lowering of the road under the offending railway bridge permitted a reversion to the original routeing in June 1966. *Dave Brown*

Above: The severe gales experienced in the autumn of 1987 are recalled by this view of RT4495 heading along Dartford Road, Sevenoaks, bound for the bus station on route 421 in August 1969; the driver has already reset the blind for the return journey to Heverham. Most of the trees in the background would be brought down in this long-remembered event, which was to destroy six of the seven trees from which the town takes its name. RT4495 had entered service in 1954, carrying a body previously on SRT95; the 160-strong SRT class attempted to marry the heavier RT body with a late STL chassis, but with the original 7.7-litre engine they proved somewhat underpowered, as well as having inadequate braking, lasting for only five years before withdrawal. RT4495 eventually met its fate in September 1976 with disposal to breakers in the Rotherham area. Route 421 has now been replaced by service 433, following a similar routeing, this being operated at the present time by Arriva Kent & Sussex. *Dave Brown*

Above: Having just left the village of Farningham, RT4047 crosses the River Darent by the Lion Hotel on route 401 (Belvedere–Sevenoaks) in August 1969. This service had started in September 1922 as East Surrey S1, running between Dartford and Sevenoaks; later extensions saw Bexleyheath added in October 1924, the service being renumbered 401 that December. The northern routeing was altered to terminate at Gravesend (Denton) in May 1934, but following local pressure the Bexleyheath terminus was reinstated in November 1935. In May 1946 the route was further extended to Upper Belvedere. Following more recent restructuring there is now no single service over the full route; Belvedere is currently served by what remains of the original service, London Central 401 from Bexleyheath, whilst Metrobus route 421 provides three weekday journeys from Sevenoaks to Farningham, terminating at Swanley, Arriva's 477 providing an onward connection to Dartford. *Dave Brown*

Right: As the Christmas crowds head for the shops in High Street, Penge, RF324, closely followed by RF318, makes its way from Crystal Palace to Chislehurst on route 227 in December 1970. In the immediate postwar era this route was operated by the well-known LT (AEC Renown) three-axle single-deckers, popularly known as 'Scooters', based at the now-closed Elmers End (ED) garage; one of this type (LT1076) survives in the care of London's Transport Museum. The RFs took over in 1952 and would continue on the route until replaced in January 1971 by SMS (AEC Swift) OMO single-deckers working from Bromley (TB) garage. RF318 would be withdrawn shortly after this photograph was taken, RF324 surviving until August 1976. Route 227 is currently operated by Stagecoach Selkent, using a long version of the ubiquitous Dennis Dart SLF single-decker. *Michael Allen*

Left: RT3054 reverses in the village of Horton Kirby prior to returning to Lower Belvedere on a 491 duty on 31 May 1971. It remains in the basic LT Country Area colour scheme but with altered fleetname to reflect the identity of the new owners. One of the first services to Horton Kirby was East Surrey route S1 (later 401), which terminated here for six months in 1923/4; from 1928 new route 401B (Dartford [Bull]–Eynsford) covered this section, only to be withdrawn itself in April 1933; it was replaced that July by service 499 (Eynsford–Erith). Further adjustments in February 1946 saw route 467 introduced between Horton Kirby and Sidcup, whilst the 491 made its way to Lower Belvedere, the services eventually splitting at Crayford. *Michael Allen*

Left: In the village of Knockholt Pound former Green Line RF117 is shown on Orpington circular route 471, having just set down a solitary passenger at the Three Horseshoes crossroads during June 1971. The LT roundel on the bus shelter is of interest in being green rather than red. The older-style signpost is still extant, although its fingerboards have now been replaced with examples of a more modern design, presumably due to local changes. RF117, also still in basic LT Country Area livery but with front roundel overpainted, was unaffected by the 1966/7 modernisation programme, having been converted for bus use in October 1965. It would be withdrawn in March 1972.
Bruce Jenkins

Above: Awaiting its next turn of duty alongside Otford's village green, with its inevitable duck pond, is RT4747 on route 421 on 18 December 1971. The village has historic associations with Thomas Becket, the 12th-century Archbishop of Canterbury martyred in his cathedral; he is reputed to have miraculously struck the source of a spring close to the local cemetery. RFs were initially allocated to route 421 in September 1953, replacing 10T10 (AEC Regal) single-deckers. Otford is still served by route 421, albeit a thrice-daily weekday (Mon-Sat) replacement running from Sevenoaks to Swanley (with schoolday extensions to Crockenhill and Wilmington), operated by Metrobus in conjunction with Southlands Travel. *Michael Allen*

Route 454 was another Autocar service acquired by the LPTB in July 1933 and, like the 402, ran between Sevenoaks and Tonbridge, albeit via Sevenoaks Weald rather than the main road. The further acquisition, in October 1939, of independent West Kent Motor Services led to an extension to Chipstead via Riverhead, the route then remaining in this form until the 1970s. RT613 is seen in Sevenoaks bus station on 18 December 1971 on a reasonably well-loaded working to Tonbridge. A number of SM-type (AEC Swift) OMO single-deckers had been introduced from July 1971 with the intention of replacing RTs but would themselves be succeeded from 1975 by Leyland Nationals. By 1981 the route had become an extremely limited service on weekdays, most journeys being replaced by the diversion via Sevenoaks Weald of Green Line route 706. These roads are now served mainly by Metrobus route 401 (Westerham–Tunbridge Wells). *Michael Allen*

In common with other local routes the 413 had its origins in a service started in May 1928 by Sevenoaks-based West Kent Motor Services; initially it terminated at Edenbridge, but this section was abandoned by London Transport following company takeover in October 1939, due to its being outside the designated LPTB area. Sevenoaks bus station is once more the location as the driver of RT4747 (illustrated previously and giving an indication of the degree of interworking involved) hurries to meet departure time to either Chipstead or Brasted; he has yet to reset his own destination blind as the conductor makes hasty adjustments to the side blind on 18 December 1971. RT4747 would be withdrawn in February 1977 and sold to Yorkshire breakers the following June; route 413 was to survive until October 1986, being replaced following deregulation by a diversion of the 483.
Michael Allen

Left: In the otherwise empty expanse of Sevenoaks bus station the driver of RCL2251, on Green Line route 704 to Tunbridge Wells, waits patiently as his passengers board for a Sunday outing on 19 March 1972. Introduced in March 1946 between Windsor and Tunbridge Wells using the 10T10 type, the service could trace its origins back to 1933 route C, operating between Tunbridge Wells and Chertsey. RCLs were introduced in June 1966, replacing RFs, which had taken over in the 1950s. Following return to its original owner in November 1978 RCL2251 would be amongst 40 of the type refurbished for use on Central London route 149 (Ponders End–Victoria), being allocated to Stamford Hill (SF) depot between June 1980 and October 1984; the end came with disposal to Barnsley-area breakers in May 1985.
Michael Allen

Right: A further view of Sevenoaks bus station, with RML2436 on a Green Line 705 relief duty to Windsor on 19 March 1972. The number blind, for some reason, has failed to include this particular service, with the result that crudely chalked figures have been added. Route 705 was introduced between Sevenoaks and Windsor on 29 May 1946, the service being operated by RF coaches from 1952. In December 1967 these were replaced by RCL double-deck coaches, based at Dunton Green (DG) and Windsor (WR) garages, which continued on the 705 until replacement in March 1972 by RP (AEC Reliance/Park Royal) OMO single-deckers. The latterly much-reduced service was withdrawn in April 1979, apart from a Sunday operation between London and Tunbridge Wells via Westerham, mainly to compensate for a lack of buses between the latter town and Bromley. RML2436 returned to LT in December 1977 but was not accepted for further service and was sent to Wombwell Diesels, near Barnsley, for breaking the following January. *Michael Allen*

Heading for the town centre on Green Line route 704, RCL2254 makes its way past the distinctive architecture of Tunbridge Wells on 19 March 1972. The town was amongst the outermost limits of LT operation, in what was predominantly Maidstone & District territory, although until December 1967 there had been a small coach garage here (code TW), along with a Green Line terminus which also closed subsequently. The RCLs were eventually succeeded by RP OMO single-deckers shortly after this photograph was taken.

Renumbered 706 in April 1979, the route's southern section was withdrawn completely by Kentish Bus in April 1990. Tunbridge Wells is still served from Bromley by a reinstated route 402, operated by Arriva Kent & Sussex with low-floor DAF SB220/Plaxton Prestige single-deckers. RCL2254 was a further example of its type renovated by LT for use on route 149; sold in 1984, it is currently privately preserved in Harrow. *Michael Allen*

Closely followed by a 'customised' Mini with widened mudguards, RT3301 heads for the centre of Sidcup on a 51A duty to Green Street Green on a sunny day in July 1972. The suffix letter was discontinued in May 1977, when the original parent route was effectively withdrawn. At the same time the RMs which had replaced the RTs on the 51A the previous January were themselves succeeded by DMS (Daimler/Leyland Fleetline) OMO double-deckers. Further alterations were effected in September 1982, when the 51 was shortened to terminate at Orpington, the section to Green Street Green (Rose & Crown) initially being covered by a diversion of route 229 from its previous terminus at Farnborough (George). RT3301 met its fate in April 1973, when it was sold to Barnsley-area breakers. *Michael Furnell*

Against a particularly fine spring sky SM519 is seen in Park Avenue, Northfleet, on 7 April 1973 on a 495 duty to King's Farm Estate. The SMs were ordered by London Transport for the Country Area just prior to its handover to NBC but were delivered to the newly formed London Country Bus Services following this change in January 1970; they were finished in the basic livery latterly adopted by LT for this sector of its services, with appropriate alterations reflecting the new ownership. The SMs were found to have mechanical shortcomings similar to those encountered with their longer MB cousins and variants, and by 1980 the majority had been withdrawn for scrapping rather than resale for further use. Route 495 now runs from the local superstore at Pepper Hill (south of Northfleet), operated by Arriva Kent Thameside. *Lyndon Rowe*

With the rather bleak surroundings in this part of Bexleyheath suggesting imminent redevelopment, RF596 prepares to make a right turn at the junction of Mayplace Road West with Erith Road (A220), on its journey to Joyce Green Hospital, Dartford, from Upper Belvedere on route 486 on 7 April 1973. The livery is that first adopted by London Country for the majority of the fleet, LT's cream relief being replaced by a canary yellow that was also used as substitute for the previous gold fleetnames and numbers. Conversion of this service to SM operation would commence officially in August 1975, RF596 being withdrawn in January 1976. *R. C. Riley*

The original Dartford (DT) garage, in Priory Road, was constructed for Maidstone & District in 1927 but was transferred to London Transport upon its formation in July 1933, along with a number of vehicles and the company's other base locally, in Old Dover Road, Northfleet. Priory Road would eventually close in January 1986, being replaced by a new depot located on an industrial site in Central Way, Dartford. Pictured on the forecourt of the original premises on 7 April 1973, RMC1499, operating from Swanley (SJ) garage, awaits its next journey to Chelsfield on route 477. Following further service as a training vehicle at Hounslow (AV) and Shepherds Bush (S) garages between 1987 and 1991, it is now used for accommodation at a go-kart circuit in Argelès-sur-Mer in southwest France. *R. C. Riley*

The residential suburb of Hayes, south of Bromley, is the location for this view of RT4583, seen heading along Hayes Garden towards Hayes Station terminus on Sundays-only route 119B during March 1974. Conversion to RMs took effect during 1975, these in turn being replaced by T (Leyland Titan) double-deckers in October 1984. The service was covered by parent route 119 from April 1985, the section along Shirley Way becoming part of route 194A. Currently operated by Metrobus using the latest Scania/East Lancs low-floor double-deckers, it now runs between the old Croydon Airport and Bromley North station. Hayes Garden is no longer used as a bus route. RT4583 was sold abroad in October 1976, to Le Nouveau Centre in Paris. *Michael Allen*

One of 175 Green Line RFs modernised in 1966/7, RF28 is pictured in Hayes on route 705 to Sevenoaks during March 1974. The upgrading programme was undertaken with the aim of presenting a more up-to-date image of the fleet, the majority of the type being then almost 15 years old. Interior alterations included red/grey seat moquette and fluorescent lighting of the type introduced on the Routemaster coaches, whilst external changes included the adoption of twin headlamps and a curved one-piece drivers windscreen; these were set off by a wide lime-green waistband with chrome trim, the overall effect being completed by black-on-yellow blinds and route-boards. Withdrawn in July 1977, RF28 was last noted with owners in Chipperfield, Herts. *Michael Allen*

With the parking meters for private cars shrouded and the relating bays given over to bus use due to the additional traffic generated, RT4781 waits at its temporary terminus in Station Road, Bromley, on 18 May 1974 on one of the many extra 410 workings to Biggin Hill for the annual Air Display weekend. The basic LT Country Area livery remains, although the radiator badge appears to have been reversed, reflecting its LCBS ownership. This event saw a considerable increase in passengers carried on the route, and additional vehicles were brought in at various times from garages other than Godstone, such as Dunton Green (DG), Northfleet (NF) and even Grays (GY), on the other side of the Thames, in Essex. RT4781 would meet its end in March 1976, at the hands of Rotherham-based breakers. *R. C. Riley*

Left: With the grounds of the local cemetery as a backdrop, RML2447 stands at the Eglinton Road terminus of route 487 in Swanscombe during August 1974, before returning to either the King's Farm Estate at Gravesend or Singlewell. It has been painted in the rather bland NBC corporate colour scheme, introduced in 1972, of leaf green with white relief, replacing the previous LCBS attractive mid-green livery with canary-yellow lining and lettering; the company's distinctive 'Flying Polo' symbol has also disappeared and been replaced by NBC's somewhat uninspiring corporate 'double N'. Converted to OMO with single-deckers in the mid-1970s, the route would be withdrawn in December 1981, the 480 timetable (amongst others) being adjusted to provide replacement. Like others of its type, RML2447 would eventually return to LT, ending its service career on route 9 when Routemaster operation by London United finished in September 2004.
Michael Allen

Above right: With several well-known High Street names evident, RF88 negotiates King Street in the centre of Gravesend on its way to the Clock Tower terminus of route 450 in August 1974; the fashion-conscious will note this was a period when 'flares' were all the rage! RF88 was one of the few of its type to appear in the approved NBC livery of leaf green, with the fleet identity displayed on the roof panels; Originally a Green Line vehicle, it had been modernised in February 1967. However, for various reasons, including unreliability caused by traffic problems and increased private-car use, these services continued to decline, and RF88 was converted for bus use in March 1972. Withdrawal would come in July 1976. *Michael Allen*

Right: A hopeful pedestrian waits to cross Milton Road, Gravesend, as RML2323 on route 480 makes slow progress along this traffic-filled thoroughfare on a damp day in August 1974. Although the destination is shown as Gravesend (Denton), the driver has neglected to reset the blind, for the bus is in fact heading in the opposite direction, probably to Erith. Following return to its original owner in July 1979, RML2323 was latterly employed on Arriva route 73 until September 2004, when the Routemasters were replaced with articulated Mercedes-Benz Citaros.
Michael Allen

Left: Route 1 has its origins in an unnumbered Vanguard service between Cricklewood and Elephant & Castle, introduced in July 1905. During the early 1920s a daily route pattern was established between Kilburn and Greenwich, later adjusted to run between Willesden and Lewisham. In the 1930s the Tilling company became involved, but the route remained much the same until 1957, when it was shortened to run from Marylebone station to Surrey Docks. Further alterations during 1965 saw it operating daily to Catford (TL) garage, with a Monday-Friday extension to Bromley (TB) garage. From October 1969 it was a basic weekday service between Marylebone and Bromley (TB) garage via the West End, eventually becoming the final RT route to serve Oxford Street and Regent Street. RT1623 is illustrated in November 1974 in Bromley High Street, bound for the garage. *Michael Allen*

Above: In February 1969 the 402 was converted from predominantly RT to RF operation. In a rural scene in London Road (A224) in Dunton Green, RF548 is shown opposite the bus garage while on route 402 from Bromley to Sevenoaks on 14 January 1975. The reduced destination display allowed one blind to list details of all related services, avoiding the need for frequent blind changes resulting from complex route interworking. The filling station, complete with original pumps and signs, has long since disappeared, having given way to residential development, but the Duke's Head, with timber-clad exterior, remains. RF548 would eventually be withdrawn from service in June 1976. *R. C. Riley*

Left: Having just passed under the Oxted–Uckfield railway line in Little Browns Lane, Troy Town (near Edenbridge), MBS270 heads for Horsham in West Sussex on 22 February 1975. Introduced by LT in April 1966, the AEC Swift OMO single-decker, in its various forms, was found to be not particularly successful in service, due to mechanical and other shortcomings, and most LCBS examples would be withdrawn by 1979. Route 434 ceased serving the Edenbridge area in August 1975, having been curtailed to terminate at East Grinstead. Metrobus currently operates an extremely limited service in Troy Town, whilst a similarly reduced service between Edenbridge and Crawley is provided by the same company's 291 route, which also serves Tunbridge Wells. *Michael Allen*

Above right: In a later view of the service provided by LCBS for the Biggin Hill Air Display (see page 37), RT4755 waits on the stand at Bromley North station on 18 May 1975 prior to picking up its next complement of passengers. It will be noted that there has been a change in the blind display since the previous year, a route number no longer being featured, whilst, unusually, fare details are now provided. This information is displayed on a paper sticker, using the blue background normally employed to indicate an 'Express' service. RT4755 would be withdrawn in September 1976, being sold to Rotherham breakers that November. *R. C. Riley*

Right: Seen on a Green Line 725 working from Windsor to Dartford, SMA17 makes its way along Croydon Road, Beckenham, on 28 May 1975. Its livery is similar to that introduced in 1966 on modernised Green Line RFs but features LCBS mid-green in lieu of LT's Lincoln green. Originating as an order diverted from South Wales Transport, the 21 SMA (AEC Swift/Alexander) coaches were purchased in 1972 for use on route 725, replacing the RFs previously employed. The service was eventually superseded in October 1986 by sister orbital route 726, introduced May 1977, running to a similar pattern but deviating via Heathrow Airport. Latterly the 726 was operated by Tellings Golden Miller as a limited-stop 'red bus' service between Heathrow and Bromley; since April 2005, renumbered X26 and cut back still further, from Bromley to East Croydon, the route has been operated by Metrobus with the latest Scania OmniCity single-deckers. *R. C. Riley*

Above: Route 404 operated from Sevenoaks to Shoreham via Otford, so it would appear that the driver of RF183, seen heading down Filston Lane, Shoreham, towards Otford on 12 June 1975, has failed to reset his blind for the return journey. The bus is pictured against the typical backcloth of a hop plantation, a well-known feature across a wide area of the county. Route 404 had its origins in a service started by independent operator Sevenoaks Motor Services in November 1929; East Surrey soon began some intensive services in competition, with the eventual result that the Sevenoaks company ceased operations in November 1930. During the 1930s the 404 was noteworthy in being operated with C-type (Leyland Cub) 20-seat single-deckers. A much-reduced timetable is now in effect with replacement route 434, amounting to three weekday return journeys provided by Arriva Kent & Sussex. *Michael Furnell*

Right: Introduced in August 1975, route 492 replaced the long-standing 467, with some variations to its previous route to Sidcup; the earlier service had been introduced in February 1946. With a London Transport DMS on route 96 and RMC1485 on route 499 bringing up the rear, SM524 leaves Westgate Road, Dartford, on route 492 to Horton Kirby in September 1975. Delivered to London Country in 1970/1, the 138 OMO single-deckers of the SM class were used to replace many of the RFs (and also some of their double-deck cousins, the RTs) on a variety of routes. As already noted, mechanical deficiencies made them unreliable, and the majority were retired after relatively short lives, generally being replaced by the standard Leyland National single-decker; most were scrapped, although some were sold overseas and others to independent operators in Hampshire. *Michael Allen*

Left: Featured in the same location as previously (and on the same date), RMC1485 makes its exit from Westgate Road on its way to Darenth Park Hospital on route 499. Of interest is the wall-mounted noticeboard, of LT design, giving directions to prospective passengers for the two hospitals in the Dartford area; both of these were later replaced by Darent Valley Hospital, in a more central location. RMC1485 returned to its original owner in February 1980, and was first employed on driver training, in similar fashion to several of its sisters, but along with six others was refurbished during 1989 for use on Express commuter route X15 (Beckton–West End); following the withdrawal of this service in 1991 it was regularly seen on sister route 15. Upon the cessation of Routemaster operation on the 15 in August 2003, it was sold to Mac Tours of Edinburgh for sightseeing work in that city. *Michael Allen*

Above: Seen north of Longfield while on a 423 working to Wrotham, RF231 makes its way along Green Street Green Road towards the village of that name on 18 September 1975. It may not be generally realised that there are two villages in northwest Kent bearing this unusual name, the other being located south of Orpington, which probably causes confusion on occasions! The route has a history stretching back to East Surrey days: having begun as the 23 (Dartford–Stanhill Farm) in January 1929, it was extended to Birchwood (Alma) in April 1930 and to Lullingstone Castle, near Eynsford, that October. Following the later absorption of M&D route 42 to Longfield and Hook Green, a through service from Swanley was inaugurated which became the 423; the Longfield–Hook Green section was eventually abandoned. Extension in 1964 from Swanley to Wrotham, over roads formerly served by the 478, saw the route assume the form in which it is illustrated here. Removal of the roadside hedge and certain trees has since altered the character of this location. *Michael Furnell*

Above: With the autumn colours highlighted by a low sun, RF183, seen previously in Shoreham, enters the village of Chelsfield on 23 October 1975 on a short working between Orpington and Knockholt Pound on route 431, which usually ran through to Sevenoaks, via Dunton Green. At this time there was routine interworking with services 402 and 471, so RF183 may have been transferring to the latter route upon arrival. The 493 was also involved in these arrangements but during this period, had a dedicated allocation of Leyland Nationals, otherwise used only on early-morning positioning journeys on the 402 and 471. *Michael Furnell*

Right: RML2340 waits on its stand at the Clock Tower on local service 498 as RML2338 passes down Harmer Street, Gravesend, on trunk route 480 from Erith on 13 April 1976. The history of route 480 is worthy of note. Introduced in 1913 by North Kent Motor Services (a subsidiary of Gravesend & Northfleet Tramways), it passed in March 1920 to Maidstone & District as route 21, running from Dartford to Gravesend. In July 1933, along with several Leylands, it was taken over by the newly formed LPTB, which renumbered it 486; the number 480 was adopted in November 1935, and an Erith extension introduced in April 1938. The basic route remains today, running between Dartford (Temple Hill) and Gravesend (Valley Drive). RML2338, having returned to LT ownership in the late 1970s, remained operational (latterly with London Central on route 12) until November 2004 and is now earmarked for the proposed Welsh Transport Heritage Museum. RML2340 was similarly retired from route 73 that September and is currently with a private owner in Slough. *R. C. Riley*

Left: RMC1483 pauses in Orpington High Street on a 477 duty bound for Chelsfield in the mid-1970s; the Commodore cinema, prominent in this view, has since been demolished. Around this time the 477 ran from Dartford to Chelsfield, via Swanley; nowadays, having been cut back to Orpington from Chelsfield, it runs to/from the Bluewater shopping complex, via the Darent Valley Hospital, and is operated by Arriva Kent Thameside. Following its return to LT in February 1980 RMC1483 was employed on driver training until withdrawn in August 1989 and scrapped at Wandsworth (WD) garage. *Dave Brown*

Above: On the final leg of its journey from Woolwich to the Farnborough (George) terminus of route 51, RT3715 makes its way towards Farnborough High Street in April 1976. The route ceased to use Farnborough as a terminus in May 1977, when its service variation 51A adopted the main route number whilst continuing to terminate at Green Street Green. RMs had been allocated to the 51 the previous June and thus saw less than a year on the original routeing. RT3715 would be taken out of service in January 1977 and sold that July to Wombwell Diesels for breaking. *Dave Brown*

Left: Pictured in Elm Road, Sidcup, on 29 May 1976 is RM191 on a short working of route 228 to Sidcup (Frognal Corner) from Eltham (Well Hall station). This bus is from the first production batch of 249 Routemasters that possessed plain upper-deck windows as a recognition feature; also evident is the plain all-white roundel, applied to the majority of the fleet from 1974 until the 1987 re-design. RM191 was to see service with two further operators subsequent to initial disposal in March 1987, first as Strathtay Scottish 622 until June 1994, when it was re-registered AST 416A, and subsequently as Reading Mainline 11, entering service there the same year. Consequent on the takeover of the company by Reading Buses, the town's main operator, RM191 returned to London in July 2000, due to Transport for London's Routemaster-expansion programme, and re-entered service on route 13

(Golders Green–Aldwych), on which it ran until the Routemasters were replaced in October 2005. *Michael Furnell*

Above: Chislehurst War Memorial is the location for RT3845 and an unidentified sister on route 161 during June 1976; both still bear the original form of underlined 'LONDON TRANSPORT' fleetname, but the relief band is now flake grey rather than cream. As the driver of RT3845 resets his destination blind an empty Green Line SMA makes its way south between duties. The RT would be withdrawn from service in May 1977 and sold to one of the Barnsley-area breakers; route 161 is still in existence at the time of writing but has been extended to North Greenwich, and current operator Metrobus employs Scania/East Lancs OmniDekkas. *Dave Brown*

Above: On a 498 duty to Northfleet (Plough), RML2339 heads along The Hill towards the town centre, having just negotiated the busy road junction opposite the well-known Leather Bottel inn, during August 1976. Following territorial adjustments London Country responsibility for this local service was to end that October upon its transfer to Maidstone & District but would be resumed in April 1978, when M&D gave up its operations in the Gravesend area. RML2339, after return to its former owner in October 1979, initially worked from Finchley (FY) garage but latterly ran for London General on routes 14 and 22 from Putney (Chelverton Road) (AF) garage, until Routemasters were replaced on these routes by WVL (Volvo B7TL/Wright) low-floor double-deckers in July 2005. *Michael Allen*

Right: Bourne Road in Dartford is the location for this view of RF221 heading towards Crayford on a 492 journey to Wilmington (Capel Place), on 18 August 1976. Route 492 had been introduced in this form in August 1975, replacing in part, route 467, which was then withdrawn; the new service was officially scheduled for SM operation, so the RF is presumably acting in substitution as a result of type unavailability. Officially demoted from Green Line to bus work in January 1967, RF221 would eventually be removed from service in March 1979. *Michael Furnell*

In the early quiet of a bright Sunday morning, on 24 October 1976, RT2250 departs Bellegrove Road, Welling, for the town's Springfield Road on a short working of route 89. At this time the service operated between Lewisham and Eltham (Well Hall station). During April 1978 this was converted to DMS type one-man-operated double-deckers, at the same time being withdrawn between Eltham and Bexleyheath and re-routed to Slade Green. The service is currently operated by London Central and now employs PVL (Volvo B7TL/Plaxton) low-floor double-deckers. In October 1978 RT2250 was sold to Mercedes-Benz, later being exported for display in the company's museum near Stuttgart. *Michael Furnell*

On 17 February 1977, a wet and dismal day, RF218 heads along Station Road, Longfield, on a short working of route 490 to the station from New Ash Green; this latter point had become the southern terminus when the service was diverted and extended from Hartley Court in July 1973. It will be observed that RF218 is still in the revised Green Line livery applied when the vehicle was modernised in May 1967, although the absence of a replacement for the Green Line totem, removed upon transfer to LCBS, presents a rather unfinished frontal appearance. Withdrawn in August 1977, it was last recorded in somewhat mundane use as a storeshed with an owner in Ewell, Surrey. *Michael Furnell*

Being overtaken by what could be considered one of the first micro-minis, a Fiat 500, SM494 leaves the stop in Instone Road, Dartford, on 19 April 1977; it was from the second batch (SM449-538) delivered to London Country, between July 1970 and June 1971, with bodywork by Metro-Cammell. Route 401 (Sevenoaks–Belvedere) was converted to the type in July 1971, replacing the RT allocations from Swanley (SJ) and Dartford (DT) garages. The service was subsequently cut back from Sevenoaks to Eynsford in January 1978, although an extension from Belvedere to Thamesmead was introduced in July 1983. The factory premises on the left of this view have now been replaced by a large car park for the Priory Centre, a shopping mall in the current fashion.
Michael Furnell

Left: Following the creation of LCBS in January 1970 one of the main priorities was to update the rather elderly fleet inherited from LT, and the first double-deck renewals came in January 1972 in the shape of 11 Daimler Fleetlines with Northern Counties bodywork, diverted from Western Welsh. All entered service that February on route 410 from Godstone (GD) garage, the RMLs from 1965 thereby being released to replace the RT type elsewhere. All were delivered in the company's pleasing livery of mid-green with yellow relief shown here. AF4 waits at the Bromley North stand, ready to depart on its return working to Reigate on 18 March 1977. The complete class remained in service, generally on the 410, for only around 10 years, the last survivor, AF6, being scrapped in 1987, after a period out of use following a spell as a driver-trainer. *R. C. Riley*

Right: Followed by a lengthy queue of traffic, RM383 heads up Sidcup Hill, towards the town centre, on a 51 duty from Farnborough to Woolwich (Hare Street). The photograph was taken on 19 May 1977 — just two days prior to the change which saw the 51 adopt the routeing of its 51A variant (which was now withdrawn), terminating at Green Street Green (Rose & Crown) rather than Farnborough (George). RM383, which had entered service in July 1960 at the former trolleybus depot at Highgate (HT), would be sold to Yorkshire breakers in September 1985, by which time it had regained its original body. *Michael Furnell*

Taken on 29 June 1977 from a high vantage-point in Dartford's Temple Hill estate, this photograph affords a view across the Dartford Marshes and River Thames and reveals some of the industrial installations on the north side of the river, in the Purfleet area of Essex. Climbing Trevithick Drive, RCL2237 is shown on route 499, which then linked Dartford's two main hospitals, at Joyce Green and Darenth Park (both now closed). The use of an RCL is noteworthy, as the Routemaster allocation at Dartford (DT) garage consisted only of the RMC type, so this was presumably a loan from elsewhere. Following return to its previous owner a refurbished RCL2237 would be operated by Edmonton (EM) garage on route 149 between October 1980 and May 1984, being sold to Yorkshire breakers the following December. *Michael Furnell*

In a traffic-free High Street (itself a sight consigned to history) in Beckenham on 15 July 1977 we find former Green Line RF221 — pictured earlier (page 55) on route 492 in its previous livery — reverting to its original role on route 725 to Windsor, substituting for one of the SMA vehicles allocated to the service at this time. The 725 was the original Green Line orbital route, introduced in July 1953; its operation would be substantially reduced by October 1984, when parallel route 726 assumed most of its traffic, and withdrawn completely in

October 1986. All of the shops depicted in this scene have now changed ownership, with the exception of that of the funeral directors, for whose services there is, no doubt, a continuing demand! The 'Three Tuns' has lost its name and is now part of a small restaurant chain, whilst the Midland Bank has been absorbed by the HSBC empire. There has also been limited rebuilding. *R. C. Riley*

Left: In the picturesque village of Downe, once the home of naturalist Charles Darwin and one of the Central Area's most rural outposts, RT1538 on route 146 commences its return journey to Bromley along Kent's narrow country lanes in April 1978. The service had its origins in the LGOC's Lewisham–Westerham Hill route of 1925, which latterly became a Thomas Tilling operation; this eventually took the form of variation 146B (Lewisham–Downe) in May 1933. Later, as the 146A, it was cut back from Lewisham to Bromley, finally losing its suffix letter in 1952. In January 1977 RMs were introduced for the Sunday duty, but both these and the RTs would be replaced by BL (Bristol LH6L) OMO single-deckers later in April 1978. The service is now operated, on weekdays only, by Metrobus, with 8.8m Dennis Dart SLFs. *Dave Brown*

Below: Close to the end of RT operation on route 94 in August 1978, RT3202 is seen approaching the stop by the Crooked Billet in Southborough Lane, Bromley, on its journey from Petts Wood to Lewisham. This establishment (now part of a national restaurant chain) had served as the terminus for the 94 until the route was extended to Petts Wood in May 1954. RT3202 is also of interest, being one of the 34 transferred back to LT by LCBS in September 1972 (and illustrated on page 30 of the author's previous album, *London Buses around Surrey*). The 94 was to be the last route south of the Thames to be converted to RM operation, on 27 August 1978. Final withdrawal of the RT type from LT service would take place on 7 April 1979 with the conversion to RM of route 62, running from Barking (BK) garage. *Roy Hobbs*

Above: The outer-London terminus of several routes, Crystal Palace Parade is illustrated here in August 1978 with a variety of vehicles, including RM, DMS and LS types. The opportunity has been taken to include this well-known venue, as its eastern side formed part of the original London/Kent boundary. A replacement bus station has since been built, and at the present time 10 services turn here, including long-running routes 3, 122, 157 and 227. Of these, the 122 served Bexleyheath before being cut back to Plumstead in January 1988, whilst the 227 continues to operate via Penge and Beckenham to Bromley North station. RM458, seen here on route 122, was withdrawn in July 1990 and sold to Barnsley breakers. *Roy Hobbs*

Right: A photograph taken at the foot of East Hill, Dartford, where a new road has been recently constructed to connect the town centre with the Bluewater shopping complex by means of the new Fastrack busway. Heading into the town centre on 19 August 1978 on a 480 working from Gravesend to Erith is RML2328, still in the attractive mid-green livery originally adopted by LCBS. Like the majority of its LCBS sisters it still bears its original body, not having passed through Aldenham for overhaul, and this situation still applies today. Having returned to LT in October 1979 it was to end its London career when replaced on route 38 (Clapton–Victoria) by Mercedes-Benz Citaro 'bendy' buses in October 2005. *Geoff Rixon*

Seen in Bromley's East Street shortly after leaving the Bromley North stand, RT1599 makes what could be a final journey on route 119, some three days before the disappearance of the type from Bromley (TB) garage on 27 August 1978. This service had officially been converted to RM operation during May 1976, so presumably RT1599 was substituting for a defective vehicle. Following withdrawal in July 1979 it found a new home at the opposite end of the country, last being recorded with an owner in Wick, in the far north of Scotland. *Michael Furnell*

Seen in the elegant suburban surroundings of Petts Wood, RM1063 passes along Chislehurst Road on a 161A duty returning to Abbey Wood (AW) garage on 24 August 1978, RMs having superseded RTs on this route in May 1977. Subsequently renumbered 161, the service would see the removal of RMs from Abbey Wood in October 1981 and a partial conversion to MD (Scania/MCW Metropolitan) double-deckers operating from the new Plumstead (PD) garage, resulting in the closure of the original Plumstead (AM) premises. Following disposal in August 1987 RM1063 passed to Wycombe Youth Council in High Wycombe but was secured for private preservation in April 1991, currently being with an owner in Richings Park, near Iver, Bucks. *Michael Furnell*

Left: Shortly after leaving St Mary Cray, RMC1492 is seen in the pleasantly rural surroundings of the B258 Crockenhill Road, by its junction with Waldens Road and close to Kevington Farm, bound for Dartford on route 477 on 4 October 1978. New to Epping (EP) garage in October 1962 for Green Line routes 718 and 720, RMC1492 would return to LT in January 1980, being first used for driver training at Hammersmith (R) garage. It subsequently passed to CentreWest, being employed both as a trainer and as a recruitment vehicle, before being sold overseas in August 1999 to Warsaw, where it is now used in a promotional capacity by an advertising agency. *Michael Furnell*

Above: Shown passing along Shepherds Lane, Dartford, is SM538 on a 486 journey from Belvedere station to the local Joyce Green Hospital on 4 October 1978. Conversion of this route from RF operation was completed in March 1976, the process having begun the previous summer. Route 486 no longer exists in this form, having been replaced in part by London Central route 401, running between Thamesmead bus centre and Bexleyheath (and recalling the previous LCBS service), and route 96, operated by Stagecoach Selkent between Woolwich and the Bluewater complex. *Michael Furnell*

Below: Having worked across outer London from Crystal Palace, RM618 is seen in Pickford Lane, Bexleyheath, bound for the terminus of route 122 at Bexleyheath (BX) garage, on 4 November 1979. Having taken over from RTs in April 1978, RMs would work this route until replaced in February 1980 by MD double-deckers. These later operated from the new Plumstead (PD) garage, which became the terminus in January 1988, when the service was cut back from Bexleyheath. At the same time new route 422, operated by London Regional Transport's then newly-formed Bexleybus subsidiary, was introduced between Bexleyheath and Woolwich; this service, now extended to North Greenwich and worked by London Central, survives today and employs PVL (Volvo B7TL/Plaxton) low-floor double-deckers. RM618, new to Highgate (HT) depot in 1961 and first used in the trolleybus-replacement programme, was sold to Barnsley breakers in August 1985. *Michael Furnell*

Right: In West Street, Gravesend, on that stretch of road bordering the River Thames and close to the Tilbury Ferry terminal, we discover the unusual sight of RMC1500 on a 480 duty to Gravesend (Valley Drive). Photographed on 13 November 1979, it had been pressed into service on this normally RML-operated route on account of a type shortage at Northfleet (NF) garage, which was compounded by the late delivery of new vehicles. The later form of NBC emblem will be noted, as will the somewhat limited blind information. RMC1500 had entered service at Garston (GR) garage in November 1962 for use on Green Line route 719 and on its return to LT in March 1981 would see further use as a training vehicle until retirement in March 1992; re-registered ALC 368A and a further two owners later, it is now privately preserved in Romford. *Michael Allen*

The now long-departed stand opposite Farnborough 'George' is illustrated here in August 1980, with RM713 awaiting departure on route 47. During September 1982, in one of the largest route restructurings carried out since the mid-1960s, the service would be revised to terminate at Bromley (TB) garage, connecting route 229 being similarly adjusted to finish at Green Street Green. The 47 has since been further cut back to Catford (TL) garage, and Farnborough is now served by Metrobus 358 (Crystal Palace–Orpington) and Arriva 402 (Bromley–Tunbridge Wells). Following sale by LT RM713 would enter service in Carlisle in October 1987 with Cumberland Motor Services (900), eventually being re-registered as TSK 270. After a spell in Italy, from June 2000, it returned to London as part of TfL's Routemaster-expansion programme, working for Arriva on route 19 from March 2004 but ending its second London career on the 159 in December 2005.
Roy Hobbs

West Wickham is the setting for RM768 as it prepares to turn from the High Street into Wickham Court Road while on route 119B from Thornton Heath to Bromley North station on Sunday 23 August 1981; Routemasters had been introduced in January 1975, replacing the RT type. The route-number suffix would be dropped in April 1985, when the separate Shirley Way section was incorporated into route 194A (Croydon Airport–Forest Hill). RM768 had entered service in April 1961 from Edmonton (EM) depot, where it was involved in the replacement of trolleybus routes 627, 659 and 679; withdrawal, from Peckham (PM) garage, would come in May 1987, to be followed by sale that October to Wigley of Carlton, Yorkshire, for breaking. *Michael Furnell*

A regular aspect of LT operations in the spring and summer months was the running of weekend staff excursions to a variety places, mainly coastal resorts in the South and South East. RM1737 of Ash Grove (AG) garage is seen in June 1981 on one such outing, probably heading for Margate, the location being the Ship Inn at Ospringe, on the A2 near Faversham. RM1737 was at this time the garage showbus, as indicated by its excellent restoration to original condition. Upon withdrawal it would be selected to represent the majority of its type in London's Transport Museum but is currently in store pending completion of the museum's renovation. *Bruce Jenkins*

Above: As a delivery van from once well-known national men's outfitters Hepworths recedes in the distance DMS2404 heads along the High Street in Welling on a 96 journey to Dartford on 15 April 1982. This service had been the replacement for trolleybus route 696 (withdrawn in March 1959) and was originally worked by RTs; in November 1971 these were succeeded by the OMO type illustrated here. Nowadays operated by Stagecoach Selkent with Dennis Trident double-deckers, the route has latterly been extended to Bluewater and runs non-stop from Dartford. *Michael Furnell*

Right: Due to a significant reduction in passenger numbers following the doubling of fares in March 1982 a large programme of service revisions was undertaken the following September. One effect was the introduction of routes 208 and 261, both operating between Lewisham and Orpington but by different routeings; together these enabled the complete withdrawal of route 94 and the abandonment of Farnborough (George) as a terminus for routes 229 and 47. Seen collecting passengers in Bromley High Street on 4 September 1982, the first day of the revised services, is RM829 of Catford (TL) garage. This bus had entered service at Stamford Hill (SF) depot in July 1961 as part of the trolleybus-replacement programme and would be withdrawn from Battersea (B) garage in February 1985, to be despatched in April to Barnsley for breaking. The route continues, currently with Dennis Trident double-deckers operated by Stagecoach Selkent. *Geoff Rixon*

Taken on the same date as the previous photograph, this picture shows RM258 on route 261, also on its first day of operation, passing along Farnborough High Street on an Orpington-bound duty, with the inevitable Mini in the background! As with other early examples of the type, RM258's first allocation was to West Ham (WH) depot in April 1960, when buses replaced the trolleybuses on routes 687, 697 and 699. Withdrawal would come in May 1987, when it was despatched to one of the Barnsley-area breakers. Following route restructuring in the Orpington area the 261 would be cut back between there and Bromley (TB) garage during August 1986; operated by Metrobus since November 1987, it now runs to Bromley Common (Crown) using East Lancs Lolyne-bodied Dennis Tridents.
Michael Furnell

The regular service through Biggin Hill was traditionally the preserve of route 410 (Reigate–Bromley via Westerham), originally East Surrey S10, introduced in June 1922. It continued operating in this guise until September 1990, when a new LRT-contracted service (320) replaced the Westerham–Bromley section; the 410 remained over the shortened original route. The newly re-branded London & Country — at the time still officially London Country (South West) — gained the weekday contract for the 320, which it worked until re-tendering, Stagecoach Selkent taking over in November 1997; this saw the return of red double-deckers to Biggin Hill for the first time since October 1948, when LT summer route 146 (Bromley–Westerham Hill) was withdrawn. Here Leyland Titan T1108 passes the well-known Black Horse inn, remembered for its Battle of Britain associations, on a Biggin Hill Valley short working on 29 May 1998. Metrobus would take over the route in September 1998, its Scania/East Lancs double-deckers now routinely ending their journey in Biggin Hill Valley.
Roy Hobbs

Although the small town of Westerham has remained virtually unchanged over the years, the pattern of local bus operation has altered considerably in recent times, and we see here the unusual sight of a red double-decker from the fringes of outer London about to return to Bromley North station on route 320. Stagecoach Selkent VA129, a Volvo Olympian/Alexander, is shown picking up passengers in Market Square before tackling the steep gradients of Westerham Hill, through the North Downs ridge, on 29 May 1998. The town is at present served by replacement route 246 operated by Metrobus, which assumed the service in September 1998 following re-tendering and employs low-floor Dennis Dart single-deckers. During the summer period this route is usually extended to Chartwell, formerly the home of Westerham's most famous resident, Sir Winston Churchill. *Roy Hobbs*

Reference has been made earlier to route 402, one of the original Kent services initiated by East Surrey, which started in August 1921 as route S2, running between Bromley and Tunbridge Wells. RTs were introduced during September 1950, the service then operating mainly between Bromley and Sevenoaks; these were succeeded in February 1969 by RFs and in LCBS days by SMs and eventually Leyland Nationals. Following removal of county support in April 1981 the route was withdrawn, Green Line 706 being revised to cater for most journeys, but reappeared in May 1987 as Kentish Bus 22.

Having reverted to its original number in April 1990, it is now operated by Arriva Kent & Sussex, which operator's 6205, a DAF DB250 with Northern Counties Palatine II body, is seen in Bromley High Street *en route* to Tunbridge Wells on 6 July 2005. As an indication of the changes that have occurred here since earlier illustrations, the High Street to the rear of the bus, between Elmfield Road and Market Square, is now completely pedestrianised, whilst a vast shopping mall, The Glades, occupies the area behind the shops on the right of this picture. *Roy Hobbs*

Index of Locations

Ian Allan PUBLISHING

Full details of Ian Allan Publishing titles can be found on
www.ianallanpublishing.com
or by writing for a free copy of our latest catalogue to:
Marketing Dept., Ian Allan Publishing,
4 Watling Drive, Hinckley, Leics LE10 3EY.

For an unrivalled range of aviation, military, transport and maritime publications, visit our secure on-line bookshop at
www.ianallansuperstore.com
or visit the Ian Allan Bookshops in

Birmingham
47 Stephenson Street, B2 4DH; Tel: 0121 643 2496;
e-mail: bcc@ianallanpublishing.co.uk
Cardiff
31 Royal Arcade, CF10 1AE; Tel: 02920 390615;
e-mail: cardiff@ianallanpublishing.co.uk
London
45/46 Lower Marsh, Waterloo, SE1 7RG;
Tel: 020 7401 2100;
e-mail: waterloo@ianallanpublishing.co.uk

Manchester
5 Piccadilly Station Approach, M1 2GH; Tel: 0161 237 9840;
e-mail: manchester@ianallanpublishing.co.uk

or through mail order by writing to:
Ian Allan Mail Order Dept.,
4 Watling Drive, Hinckley LE10 3EY.
Tel: 01455 254450.
Fax: 01455 233737.
e-mail: midlandbooks@compuserve.com